FABULOUS
FISH

FABULOUS
FISH

FRESH FROM THE SEA:
50 FISH AND SHELLFISH RECIPES

LIZ TRIGG

Photography by Michelle Garrett

HERMES
HOUSE

This edition published in 1998 by Hermes House
27 West 20th Street, New York, NY 10011

HERMES HOUSE books are available for bulk purchase for sales promotion
and for premium use. For details, write or call the sales director,
Hermes House, 27 West 20th Street, New York, NY 10011;
(800) 354-9657

Hermes House is an imprint of
Anness Publishing Inc.

ISBN 1-84038-133-7

Publisher: Joanna Lorenz
Editor: Joanne Rippin
Designer: Peter Laws
Photographer: Michelle Garrett

Printed and bound in Hong Kong

1 3 5 7 9 10 8 6 4 2

CONTENTS

INTRODUCTION

Fish and shellfish are a rich source of a group of essential nutrients sometimes referred to as "brain food". They play an important role in establishing and maintaining a healthy diet, and consumers are becoming increasingly aware of the benefits of utilizing the delicious range of fresh and saltwater fish available.

Medical research has established the need to reduce the levels of fat and cholesterol in our diet. There is increasing evidence that a diet which is high in seafood contributes to a lowering of cholesterol levels, and there is also evidence that fish oil guards against hardening of the arteries and may assist in reducing the incidence of breast cancer.

These health benefits, along with the increasing varieties of fish now available from around the world due to good, fast chilling and freezing practices, make it the ideal food on which to base an interesting and healthy diet.

Fish is one of the quickest sources of animal protein to cook, and many dishes are simple to produce. Most people's concern when cooking fish is with the preparation, but the skills of scaling, trimming, and gutting are easily mastered, and once you have done so there are endless ways of cooking it. Checking the quality of the fish when buying it, and asking the fishmonger for advice and guidance will give you confidence in choosing from the wide selection available.

Fillets of fish are a good way of incorporating fish into the diets of children and the elderly who might find the skin and bones of fish difficult to cope with.

This book aims to help you enjoy the harvest of our seas and rivers with fish cooked in many different ways based on ideas from all over the world.

Types of Fish

Crustaceans

These include shrimp, crabs and lobsters. All crustaceans have firm, sweet flesh. Most are cooked by poaching. Shrimp are delicious when sautéed in garlic butter or coated with butter and deep-fried. Lobsters are better delicately poached in a sauce or soup.

Shellfish

Some shellfish, especially oysters, should be eaten raw in their own juices from the shell. Cockles and razor clams can be eaten raw but are also good in soups too. Mussels and clams are delicious steamed in their own juices or in white wine and lemon juice and scallops are often seared on a hot griddle. Periwinkles and whelks are boiled in their own shells and served with lemon juice.

Flat fish

Sole and halibut belong to this group. They both have firm yet tender flesh. Halibut, the largest flat fish is always sold in fillets or in steaks. It has a tendency to dryness so keep it moistened during cooking. Like other small flat fish, lemon sole, sand dab and flounder can be cooked whole or filleted. Their shallow bodies make them easier to broil or sauté.

Round fish

This section includes salmon. Trout are freshwater fish, and the herring and cod families which have a more oily flesh are salt-water fish. The sprat, anchovy and sardine are included in the herring and cod family and are delicious broiled, fried or poached. Whiting has an especially delicate flavor and fine texture. Haddock is similar to cod but has a closer-grained flesh.

Storage

Shellfish deteriorate more rapidly than fish. They are therefore sold alive or sometimes, in the case of lobsters and crab, cooked. As a general rule shellfish can be recognized as fresh by their lack of smell.

Seafood will keep fresh for no more than a day if stored in the refrigerator. Loosely wrap in wax paper or foil to prevent its smell from penetrating into other foods.

When choosing fish it is the appearance and odor that reflect its condition. When buying whole fish look for shining skin, pink gills and full bright eyes with black pupils and transparent corneas. The flesh should be soft but springy. Genuinely fresh fish has a clean pleasant odor, so reject any that have even the suggestion of a "fishy smell". Exceptions to this rule are shark and skate whose flesh contains a chemical called urea which breaks down on death to cause ammonia. The smell of ammonia should not worry the cook. Just make sure that you do not cook the skate or shark immediately after catching it – it is better to store for a couple of days beforehand.

Equipment

a blunt knife. Best done under running water.

Large fish slice
Useful for lifting whole fish lengthways.

Fish slice
Good for lifting fish fillets or single portions of fish.

Fish platter
A large flat platter essential for the displaying of whole fish. It makes an attractive centerpiece.

Filleting knife
A long flexible knife is essential for skinning and filleting fish as it can curve around the shape of the fish, its bones and flesh. Keep the knife as sharp as possible.

Strong scissors
Good for trimming fins and tails.

Oyster knife
An essential knife for opening tightly closed oyster shells. They are prised apart with its small strong blade.

Zester
A quick method to add citrus fruit zest to any stuffing or marinade or as a quick fresh garnish.

Skewers
Use for brochettes to cook on the barbecue or under the broiler.

Fish-shaped mousse mould
An attractive way to present a cold mousse.

Clockwise from top left.

Fish grill for barbecuing
Ideal for small whole fish. Place the fish in the shaped grid and barbecue, turning the whole grid over half-way through the cooking time.

Fish poacher
Used to poach large whole fish. Place the fish on the trivet with water beneath. Use the tightly fitting lid to poach over two gas rings or in the oven.

Whole fish grill for barbecueing
Ideal for whole large fish. Gut before cooking and season well. Wrap in large sprigs of fresh herbs such as rosemary. Turn over half-way through the cooking time.

Fish terrine mold
Ideal for large fish pâtés or terrines. Always cook in a bain-marie, i.e., placed in a large roasting pan and filled halfway up the side of the terrine mold with boiling water. Cast iron terrine

molds like this one are ideal for cooking the terrine but always cover with the lid and line the mold with waxed paper to allow for ease of turning out. Serve the terrine sliced.

Divided fish lifter
A useful gadget which opens out so you can lift a whole or large piece of fish with one hand.

Scaler
Wonderful for scraping off those stubborn scales. Alternatively use

10

PREPARATION TECHNIQUES

Trimming Round Fish

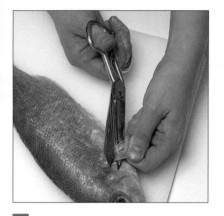

1 With a pair of heavy scissors, cut away the fins on either side of the fish then cut away the belly fins.

2 Cut away the dorsal fins along the back.

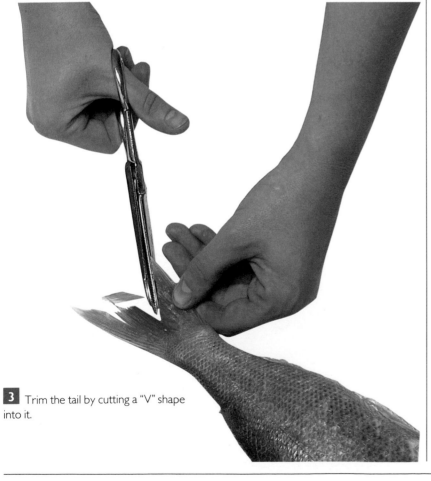

3 Trim the tail by cutting a "V" shape into it.

Gutting Through the Stomach

1 With a medium knife, slit the underside from the gills to the small ventral opening, taking care not to insert the knife too far.

2 With your fingers, carefully loosen the stomach contents from the cavity and pull them out.

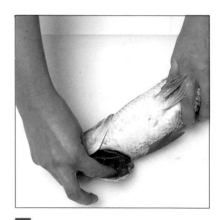

3 With a teaspoon, scrape along the vertabrae in the cavity to remove the kidney.

4 With your fingers, pull out the gills. Clean the cavity by washing away any blood.

Gutting a Round Fish

A Rapid Way to Skin Flat Fish

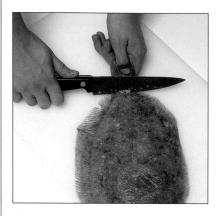 

1 Lay the fish dark side uppermost. With a sharp knife held at an angle, cut across the skin where the tail joins the body taking care not to cut all the way through.

2 With the knife still held at an angle, start to cut. Keep the fish secure on the board with some salt and gradually prise the flap of skin away from the flesh. When you have a good flap of skin, grasp the skin with your hand and hold the other end of the fish with your other hand. Firmly pull the skin towards the head.

1 With a heavy pair of scissors, cut along the fish's belly.

2 Remove the insides.

Scaling a Fish

With a fish scaler, curry comb or serrated knife held at an angle, scrape off the scales, working from tail to head. Rinse the fish regularly under cold water.

Boning Flatfish

1 Using a flexible knife, cut along the backbone.

2 Cut the flesh away from the bones, holding the knife almost parallel to them.

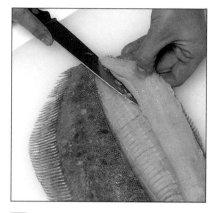

3 Cut to the edge of the transverse bones, but do not remove the fillet completely.

4 Turn the fish over and repeat for the opposite fillet.

5 Fold both fillets out.

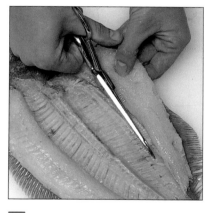

6 Using a strong pair of scissors, cut the bones along the edges.

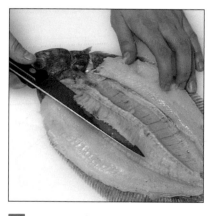

7 Loosen the bones away from the flesh.

8 With the scissors, snip the spine at the head and tail ends.

9 Lift the backbone at the tail end and pull, stripping it from the flesh underneath.

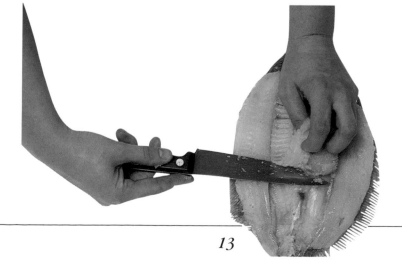

COOK'S TIP
For cooking and stuffing, lay the fish flat, and curl the top fillets back to expose the flesh underneath. To cook the fillets separately, remove completely from the sides and cut into two whole fillets.

Raw Salmon Sushi Rolls

A quite complicated starter which needs to be made with very fresh fish. Try to buy green wasabi powder to mix with water and serve with the soy sauce and pickled ginger. It will give a very authentic taste.

Serves 4

INGREDIENTS
1½ cups short grain rice
3¼ in piece of konbu seaweed
1 tbsp of sake or dry white wine
12 oz salmon fillet, skinned
1 cucumber, peeled
5 sheets of nori
2 tsp sliced pickled (optional)
  ginger
1 small jar of salmon roe
2½ tbsp rice vinegar
1 tbsp sugar
salt and freshly ground black pepper
wasabi, for dipping
soy sauce, for dipping

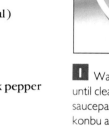
rice

nori

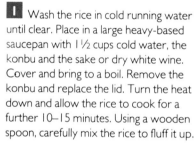
cucumber

salmon fillet

seaweed

pickled ginger

1 Wash the rice in cold running water until clear. Place in a large heavy-based saucepan with 1½ cups cold water, the konbu and the sake or dry white wine. Cover and bring to a boil. Remove the konbu and replace the lid. Turn the heat down and allow the rice to cook for a further 10–15 minutes. Using a wooden spoon, carefully mix the rice to fluff it up.

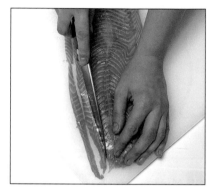

2 Transfer the rice to a shallow bowl. Leave to cool slightly. Cover with a damp dish towel to prevent the rice from drying.

3 Cut the salmon and cucumber into long strips. Lay the nori out flat on a dry dish towel.

4 Spoon a thin line of sushi rice across the width of the nori, leaving 2 in of the nori clear. Then lay a line of the salmon, cucumber, pickled ginger, salmon roe and vinegar, sugar and seasoning across the top. Top with more sushi rice.

5 Fold over the end of the nori, then using the dish towel, roll tightly. Leave for 10 minutes, unwrap, then cut into 1¼ in lengths. Repeat with the remaining ingredients. Serve with wasabi and soy sauce.

Deep-fried Whitebait

A spicy coating on these fish gives this favourite dish a crunchy bite.

Serves 6

INGREDIENTS
1 cup flour
½ tsp curry powder
½ tsp ground ginger
½ tsp ground cayenne pepper
pinch of salt
2½ lb fresh or frozen whitebait, thawed
vegetable oil for deep-frying
lemon wedges, to garnish

cayenne pepper

ground ginger

curry powder

lemon

whitebait

I Mix together all the dry ingredients in a large bowl.

2 Coat the fish in the flour.

3 Heat the oil in a large, heavy-based saucepan until it reaches a temperature of 375°F. Fry the whitebait in batches for 2–3 minutes until the fish is golden and crispy.

4 Drain well on absorbent paper towels. Serve hot garnished with lemon wedges.

Sesame Shrimp Toasts

Serve about four triangles each with a soy sauce dip.

Serves 6

INGREDIENTS
6 oz peeled shrimp
2 scallions, finely chopped
1 in ginger root, peeled and
    grated
2 garlic cloves, crushed
2 tbsp cornstarch
2 tsp soy sauce, plus extra for
    dipping
6 slices stale bread from a small loaf,
    crusts removed
3 tbsp sesame seeds
approx. 2½ cups vegetable oil for
    deep-frying

shrimp

ginger

soy sauce

garlic

scallions

sesame seeds

COOK'S TIP

Frozen shrimp tend to become fairly
soggy when defrosted, so squeeze out
any excess moisture and pat dry on
absorbent paper towels.

To check that the oil is at the right
temperature, toss a stale bread cube
into the oil. If it turns golden in 30
seconds the temperature is just right.

1 Place the shrimp, scallions, ginger and
garlic cloves into a food processor fitted
with a metal blade. Add the cornstarch
and soy sauce to work the ingredients
into a thick paste.

2 Spread the bread slices evenly with
the paste and cut into triangles. Sprinkle
with the sesame seeds and make sure
they stick to the bread. Chill for 30
minutes.

3 Heat the oil for deep-frying in a large
heavy-based pan until it reaches a
temperature of 375°F. Using a slotted
spoon, lower the toasts into the oil,
sesame seed side down, and fry for 2–3
minutes, turning over for the last minute.
Drain on absorbent paper towels. Keep
the toasts warm while frying the
remainder.

4 Serve the toasts with the soy sauce
for dipping.

Spicy Barbecued Salmon

If you intend to barbecue the salmon, make sure the barbecue is heated up thoroughly before you start to cook. It should take the same cooking time as conventional broiling.

Serves 4

INGREDIENTS
1 small red onion
1 garlic clove
6 plum tomatoes
2 tbsp butter
3 tbsp tomato ketchup
2 tbsp Dijon mustard
2 tbsp dark brown sugar
1 tbsp honey
1 tsp ground cayenne pepper
1 tbsp ancho chili powder
1 tbsp ground paprika
1 tbsp Worcestershire sauce
4 × 6 oz salmon fillets

cayenne pepper

Dijon mustard

dark brown sugar

plum tomato

red onion

salmon fillet

tomato ketchup

1 Finely chop the red onion and finely dice the garlic.

2 Dice the tomatoes.

3 Melt the butter in a large, heavy-based saucepan and gently cook the onion and garlic until translucent.

4 Add the tomatoes and simmer for 15 minutes.

5 Add the remaining ingredients except the salmon and simmer for a further 20 minutes. Process the mixture in a food processor fitted with a metal blade and leave to cool.

6 Brush the salmon with the sauce and chill for at least 2 hours. Barbecue or broil for about 2–3 minutes either side, brushing on the sauce when necessary.

Ceviche

This is a hot and sweet starter of marinated fresh fish. Take very special care in choosing the fish for this dish; it must be as fresh as possible and served on the same day it is made.

Serves 6

INGREDIENTS
12 oz medium cooked shrimp
12 oz scallops, removed from their
    shells, with corals intact if possible
12 oz salmon fillet
6 oz tomatoes
1 × 6 oz mango
1 red onion, finely chopped
1 fresh red chili
juice of 8 limes
2 tbsp sugar
2 pink grapefruits
3 oranges
4 limes
salt and freshly ground black pepper

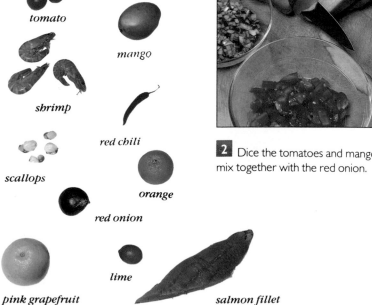

tomato

mango

shrimp

red chili

scallops

orange

red onion

lime

pink grapefruit

salmon fillet

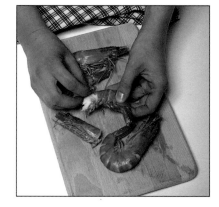

1 Peel the shrimp and cut the scallops into ½ in dice.

2 Dice the tomatoes and mango and mix together with the red onion.

3 Cut the fish into small pieces, dice the chili and mix with the fish, tomato and mango. Add the lime juice, sugar and seasoning. Stir and leave to marinate for 3 hours.

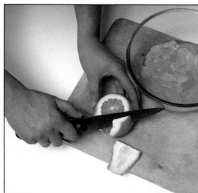

4 Segment the grapefruit, oranges and limes. Drain off as much excess lime juice as possible and mix the fruit segments into the marinated ingredients. Season to taste and serve.

Welsh Rarebit with Anchovies

A classic snack or starter adapted to include salty anchovies. Make as required because the sauce will not keep for long.

Serves 4

INGREDIENTS
1½ oz canned anchovies, drained
¾ cup butter
6 slices of bread, crusts removed
4 large egg yolks
1¼ cups heavy cream
salt and freshly ground black pepper
pinch of cayenne pepper
1 tbsp chopped fresh parsley, to garnish

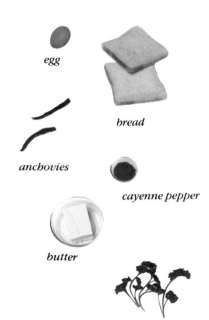

egg

bread

anchovies

cayenne pepper

butter

parsley

1 In a food processor fitted with a metal blade, process the anchovy fillets with two-thirds of the butter. Toast the bread, spread with the anchovy butter, and keep warm.

2 Melt the remaining butter in a small, heavy-based saucepan and beat in the egg yolks.

3 Take off the heat and add the cream. Season to taste then replace on a low heat. Stir continuously until you have a thick sauce. Pour over the toast and sprinkle with the cayenne. Garnish with the chopped fresh parsley.

Steamed Crab Won Ton

Won ton wrappers are available fresh from Oriental stores. They can be frozen and used as required. They can also be deep-fried for a very crispy outer coating.

Serves 6

INGREDIENTS
1 lb raw shrimp
8 oz fresh or canned crabmeat
9 oz minced pork
2 tsp water chestnuts
2 tbsp bamboo shoots
4 scallions, finely chopped
1 in piece of fresh ginger root
1 tbsp light soy sauce, plus extra for
   dipping
1 tbsp rice wine or dry sherry
1 egg white
1 package of won ton skins
1 oz frozen peas, thawed

crab

water chestnuts

bamboo shoots

won ton skins

soy sauce

scallions

peas

shrimp

pork

ginger

1 Peel and devein the shrimp.

2 Mix the crabmeat, pork, water chestnuts, bamboo shoots and scallions together.

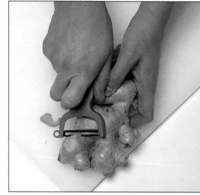

3 Peel and grate the fresh ginger.

4 Add the ginger, soy sauce, rice wine or dry sherry and egg white until the mixture becomes a thick paste.

5 Spoon 1 tsp of the mixture onto each won ton skin, gather up the sides and press gently with your fingertips to form a pouch.

6 Place a pea on top of each dumpling and wrap in small pieces of wax paper. Steam for 20 minutes. Serve with soy sauce for dipping.

Smoked Salmon Pâté

Making this pâté in individual ramekins wrapped in extra smoked salmon gives an extra special presentation. Taste the mousse as you are making it as some people prefer more lemon juice and seasoning.

Serves 4

INGREDIENTS
¾lb thinly sliced smoked salmon
⅔ cup heavy cream
finely grated rind and juice of 1 lemon
salt and freshly ground black pepper
melba toast, to serve

smoked salmon

lemon

black pepper

salt

1 Line four small ramekin dishes with plastic wrap. Line the dishes with 4 oz of the smoked salmon cut into strips long enough to flop over the edges.

2 In a food processor fitted with a metal blade, process the rest of the salmon with the seasoning, heavy cream and lemon rind and juice.

3 Pack the lined ramekins with the smoked salmon pâté and wrap over the loose strips of salmon. Cover and chill for 30 minutes, then turn out of the molds and serve with melba toast.

COOK'S TIP

Process the salmon in short bursts until it is just smooth. Don't over-process the pâté or it will thicken too much.

Grilled New Zealand Mussels with Cumin

Large New Zealand mussels have a more distinctive flavor than the more common small black variety. If you can't find these the black mussels are also delicious prepared this way.

Serves 4

INGREDIENTS
3 tbsp fresh parsley
3 tbsp fresh coriander
1 garlic clove, crushed
pinch of ground cumin
2 tbsp unsalted butter,
   softened
3 tbsp brown bread crumbs
freshly ground black pepper
12 green mussels or 24 small mussels
   on the half-shell
chopped fresh parsley, to garnish

butter

parsley

garlic

bread

coriander

mussels

1 Chop the herbs finely.

2 Beat the garlic, herbs, cumin and butter together with a wooden spoon.

3 Stir in the bread crumbs and freshly ground black pepper.

4 Spoon a little of the mixture onto each mussel and broil for 2 minutes. Serve with chopped fresh parsley.

Salt Cod Bites with Aioli

Based on a popular Spanish dish, these salty bites go very well with a strong garlicky mayonnaise. Soak the salt cod thoroughly and do not add any extra salt while preparing the dish!

Serves 4

INGREDIENTS
8 oz dried salt cod
1½ lb potatoes
1 garlic clove, crushed
3 tbsp chopped fresh parsley
1 egg yolk, beaten
1 tbsp flour
vegetable oil for deep-frying
freshly ground black pepper

For quick aioli (garlic mayonnaise)
3 garlic cloves, crushed
juice of ½ lemon
1¼ cups mayonnaise

mayonnaise

egg

salt cod

lemon

potato

garlic

parsley

1 Soak the cod for at least 24 hours, changing the water regularly.

2 Break the cod into small pieces, removing any skin or bones.

3 Cook the potatoes until tender and drain. Mash with the garlic, parsley and egg yolk.

4 Fold in the cod and season well with the freshly ground pepper. Using floured hands, shape the mixture into twenty walnut-sized balls.

5 Heat the oil in a large, heavy-based saucepan and test with a piece of stale bread to see if it is ready (see Cook's Tip, page 25). Deep-fry the balls in batches for 2 minutes or until golden brown. Drain on absorbent paper towels. Keep warm.

6 For the aioli, whisk together the garlic, lemon juice and mayonnaise. Serve with the hot fish balls.

Clam Chowder

Canned clams if necessary, once drained, can be used as an alternative to fresh ones in their shells. During cooking, if any of the clam shells remain closed, discard them as they would have been dead before cooking.

Serves 4

INGREDIENTS
1¼ cups heavy cream
6 tbsp unsalted butter
1 small onion, finely chopped
   (optional)
1 apple, sliced
1 garlic clove, crushed
3 tbsp mild curry powder
12 oz baby corn
2½ cups fish stock
8 oz new potatoes, peeled and
   cooked
24 pearl onions, peeled and boiled
40 small clams
salt and freshly ground black pepper
8 lime wedges, to garnish

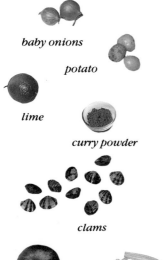

baby onions

potato

lime

curry powder

clams

apple

baby corn

1 Pour the cream into a small saucepan and cook over a high heat until it is reduced by half.

2 In a larger pan, melt half the butter. Add the onion, apple, garlic clove and curry powder. Sauté until the onion is translucent. Add the reduced cream and stir well.

3 In another saucepan, melt the remaining butter and add the baby corn. Cook for 5 minutes. Increase the heat and add the cream mixture and stock. Bring to a boil.

4 Add the potatoes, pearl onions and clams. Cover and cook until the clams have opened. Discard any that do not open. Season well to taste, and serve garnished with lime wedges.

Lobster Bisque

The blue and black clawed lobster is known as the king of the shellfish. When cooked it turns brilliant red in color. This is an extravagent soup, worthy of a special dinner party.

Serves 4

INGREDIENTS
1 live lobster 1½ lb
2 tbsp vegetable oil
115 g/4 oz butter
2 shallots, finely chopped
juice of ½ lemon
3 tbsp brandy
1 bay leaf
1 parsley sprig
blade of mace
5 cups fish stock
3 tbsp flour
3 tbsp heavy cream
salt and freshly ground black pepper
pinch of cayenne pepper, to garnish

bay leaf

cayenne pepper

lemon

shallot

lobster

parsley

1 Pre-heat the oven to 350°F. Kill the lobster. Lay the lobster flat out and split in half lengthwise. Remove and discard the little stomach sac from the head, the thread-like intestine and the coral (if any).

Pour the juices and the shell into a large saucepan and simmer with the bay leaf, parsley, mace and stock for 30 minutes. Strain. Finely chop 1 tbsp of lobster meat. Process the rest of the meat with 3 tbsp butter.

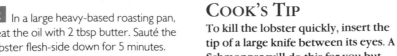

2 In a large heavy-based roasting pan, heat the oil with 2 tbsp butter. Sauté the lobster flesh-side down for 5 minutes. Add the shallots, lemon juice and brandy then put it into the preheated oven for 15 minutes. Remove the meat from the shell.

COOK'S TIP

To kill the lobster quickly, insert the tip of a large knife between its eyes. A fishmonger will do this for you but you must cook the lobster on the same day.

3 Melt the remaining butter, add the flour and cook gently for 30 seconds. Add the stock gradually and bring to a boil, stirring constantly. Stir in the meat, cream, seasoning and serve with lobster pieces and a sprinkling of cayenne.

The Ultimate Fish and Chips

This fish batter is very light and crispy and the standing time is an essential part of the result. Do not bother to peel the potatoes for the chips as the peel contains more nutrients and gives a crispier crunch. Vary the herbs you use in this traditional dish. Substitute the cod with sole or haddock if you wish.

Serves 4

INGREDIENTS
1 cup flour
1 tbsp olive oil
2 eggs, separated
2 tbsp chopped fresh herbs
4 × 6 oz cod fillets
vegetable oil, for deep-frying
8 large potatoes
salt and freshly ground black pepper

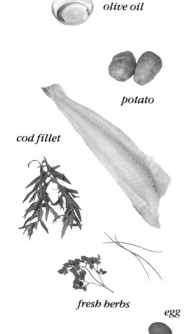

olive oil

potato

cod fillet

fresh herbs

egg

1 Sift the flour and seasoning into a large mixing bowl.

2 Whisk the olive oil with ½ cup water and the egg yolks to make a smooth batter.

3 Stir in the mixed herbs and leave to stand for at least 30 minutes.

4 Whisk the egg whites until stiff and fold into the mixture.

5 Heat the oil in a large, heavy-based saucepan and test with a piece of stale bread (see Cook's Tip, page 25). Dip the fish fillets into the batter and deep-fry for 4–7 minutes until golden brown. Drain well on absorbent paper towels and keep warm.

6 Meanwhile, make the chips. Leaving the skin on, cut the potatoes into wedges and deep-fry for 10 minutes until golden brown and crispy.

Red Mullet in Banana Leaves

Watch out for the bones in red mullet as there tend to be a lot of them. Red mullet is hard to find but worth looking for as the flavor is exceptional.

Serves 4

INGREDIENTS
8 small red mullet or kingfish, about
   6 oz each
4 sprigs fresh rosemary
banana leaves or wax paper
30 ml/2 tbsp olive oil
salt and freshly ground black pepper

rosemary

banana leaves

olive oil

red mullet

1 Preheat the oven to 425°F. Wash, scale and gut the fish.

2 Lay the fresh rosemary inside the cavity of each fish.

3 Cut a piece of banana leaf or wax paper large enough to wrap up each fish.

4 Drizzle each one with a little olive oil.

5 Season each fish well.

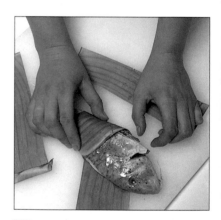

6 Wrap each fish tightly with the seam of the packet on the underside. Bake for about 12 minutes in the preheated oven and unwrap to serve.

Shrimp and Mint Salad

Shrimp make all the difference to this salad, as the flavors marinate well into the shrimp before cooking. Garnish with shavings of fresh coconut for a tropical topping.

Serves 4

INGREDIENTS
12 large shrimp
1 tbsp unsalted butter
1 tbsp fish sauce
juice of 1 lime
3 tbsp thin coconut milk
1 tsp sugar
1 garlic clove, crushed
1 in piece of ginger root, peeled and grated
2 fresh red chilies, seeded and finely chopped
freshly ground black pepper
2 tbsp fresh mint leaves
½ head light green lettuce leaves, to serve

lime
red chili
shrimp
fish sauce
coconut milk
mint

ginger *lettuce*

1 Peel the shrimp leaving the tails intact.

2 Remove the vein.

3 Melt the butter in a large frying pan and toss in the shrimp until they turn pink.

4 Mix the fish sauce, lime juice, coconut milk, sugar, garlic, ginger, chilies and pepper together.

5 Toss the warm shrimp into the sauce with the mint leaves. Serve the shrimp mixture on a bed of green lettuce leaves.

VARIATION
The shrimp can be substituted with lobster tails if you are feeling extravagant.

Fish Curry

Any mixture of white fish works well with this fresh curry. Serve with warm naan bread to mop up the delicious juices.

Serves 4

INGREDIENTS
1½ lb white boneless fish such as
   halibut, cod, pollock or monkfish
juice of ½ lime
2 tsp cider vinegar
4 cups grated fresh
   coconut
1 in piece of ginger root, peeled and
   grated
6 garlic cloves
1 lb tomatoes, chopped
3 tbsp sunflower oil
¾ lb onions, roughly chopped
20 curry leaves
1 tsp ground coriander
½ tsp ground turmeric
2 tsp ground chili
½ tsp fenugreek seeds
½ tsp cumin seeds
salt and freshly ground black pepper
banana leaves, to serve
lime slices, to garnish

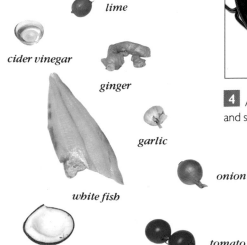

lime

cider vinegar

ginger

garlic

onion

white fish

tomato

fresh coconut

1 Marinate the fish in lime juice, vinegar and a pinch of salt for 30 minutes.

2 In a food processor fitted with a metal blade, process the grated coconut, ginger, garlic cloves and tomatoes to make a paste.

3 Heat the oil in a frying pan, add the onions and cook until golden brown, then add the curry leaves.

4 Add the coriander, turmeric and chili and stir-fry for 1 minute.

5 Add the coconut paste and cook for 3–4 minutes, constantly stirring. Pour in 1¼ cups water, bring to the boil, and simmer for 4 minutes.

6 Pound the fenugreek and cumin seeds together in a pestle and mortar. Lay the fish on top of the simmering sauce, sprinkle over the fenugreek mixture and cook for 15 minutes or until the fish is tender. Serve on banana leaves and garnish with lime slices.

Sea Bass en Papillote

A dramatic presentation to delight your guests. Bring the unopened packages to the table and let them unfold their own fish to release the delicious aroma.

Serves 4

INGREDIENTS
4 small sea bass, gutted
½ cup butter
1 lb spinach, washed well
3 shallots, finely chopped
4 tbsp white wine
4 bay leaves
salt and freshly ground black pepper

white wine

bay leaves

sea bass

shallots

butter

spinach

1 Preheat the oven to 350°F. Season both the inside and outside of the fish. Melt 4 tbsp of the butter in a large, heavy-based saucepan and add the spinach. Cook gently until the spinach has broken down into a smooth purée. Set aside to cool.

2 Melt another 4 tbsp of the butter in a clean pan and add the shallots. Gently sauté for 5 minutes until soft. Add to the spinach and leave to cool.

3 Stuff the insides of the fish with the spinach filling.

4 For each fish, fold a large sheet of wax paper in half and cut around the fish laid on one half, to make a heart shape when unfolded. It should be at least 2 in larger than the fish. Melt the remaining butter and brush a little onto the paper. Set the fish on one side of the paper.

5 Add a little wine and a bay leaf to each package.

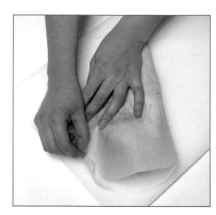

6 Fold the other side of the paper over the fish and make small pleats to seal the two edges, starting at the curve of the heart. Brush the outsides with butter. Transfer the packages to a baking sheet and bake for 20–25 minutes until the packages are brown. Serve with baby potatoes and glazed carrots.

Monkfish, Salmon and Sole Mousseline

This is a very rich fish dish. Serve as soon as possible after cooking so it is just warm.

Serves 4

INGREDIENTS
½ lb monkfish, removed from the
    bone
½ lb sole fillets
2 egg whites
1 cup heavy cream
½ tsp grated fresh nutmeg
¾ lb fresh salmon fillet
1 oz spinach
salt and freshly ground white pepper

For the sauce
1 lb tomatoes

cream

tomato

egg

sole fillets

salmon fillet

spinach

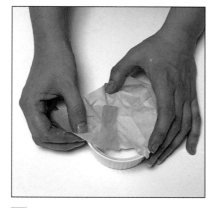

1 Preheat the oven to 350°F. Line the ramekins.

2 In a food processor fitted with a metal blade, chop the monkfish and sole with the egg white until the mixture is smooth and firm. Chill for 10 minutes.

3 Stir in the salt, pepper and nutmeg. Transfer the mixture to a large mixing bowl and place over a bowl of ice. Gradually beat in the cream, a tablespoon at a time, and chill for 30 minutes. The mixture should not be too soft – it should be thick and firm enough to hold its own shape.

4 Blanch the spinach leaves in a large heavy-based saucepan, and refresh under cold water.

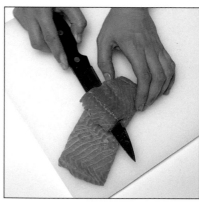

5 Cut the salmon into thin slices. Line the bases of the ramekins with a slice of salmon.

COOK'S TIP

Monkfish usually has its dark outer skin removed before sale. We buy the tail part of the monkfish which consists of one central cartilage bone and two fillets. The thin membrane has to be cut off by the cook. Cut away from the flesh with a sharp knife and pull off.

6 Layer with spinach and mousseline mixture and finish with a layer of salmon. Cover with a piece of wax paper with a pleat in the middle to allow for expansion. Place in a large roasting pan with boiling water poured in to come half way up the sides of the tin. Place in the preheated oven and bake for 20 minutes. Broil the tomatoes until the skins are blackened. Peel, then place in the food processor and purée. Season well and serve with the warm mousseline turned out of the ramekins.

Barbecued Salmon with Red Onion Marmalade

Salmon barbecues well but make sure it is at least 2.5 cm/1 in thick to make it easy to turn when cooking. The red onion marmalade is rich and delicious. Substitute a tablespoon of pureed blackcurrants for the blackcurrant liqueur if you like.

Serves 4

INGREDIENTS
4 salmon steaks, cut 1 in thick, no
    thinner
2 tbsp olive oil
salt and freshly ground black pepper

For the red onion marmalade
5 medium red onions, peeled
4 tbsp butter
¾ cup red wine vinegar
¼ cup blackcurrant liqueur
¼ cup grenadine
¼ cup red wine

red wine

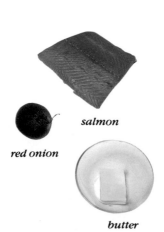
salmon

red onion

butter

1 Rub the olive oil into the fish flesh.

2 Season the fish well with salt and pepper.

3 Finely slice the onions.

4 Melt the butter in a large heavy-based saucepan and add the onions. Sauté for 5 minutes.

5 Stir in the vinegar, cassis, grenadine and wine and continue to cook until the liquid has reduced. It should take about 10 minutes until the liquid has almost entirely evaporated and the onions are glazed. Season well.

6 Brush the fish with a little more oil, and barbecue or broil for 4 minutes on either side.

Gravadlax

The freshness of the fish is important as the salmon is marinated not cooked. This is a classic dish which must always be accompanied by the traditional mustard sauce.

Serves 12 as a starter

INGREDIENTS
2½ lb salmon, head, tail and bones
    removed
3 tbsp coarse sea salt
1 oz sugar
12 crushed black peppercorns
large bunch of dill, chopped

For the mustard sauce
2 egg yolks
2 tbsp white wine vinegar
3 tbsp mild mustard
2 oz soft brown sugar
1¼ cups olive oil
2 tbsp chopped fresh dill
salt and freshly ground white pepper

olive oil

brown sugar

salmon fillet

sea salt

mustard   *white wine vinegar*

dill

I Place one of the fillets skin-side down on a non-metallic platter. Sprinkle over the coarse salt, sugar and crushed black peppercorns. Cover with half of the dill.

2 Lay the other fillet on top with the remaining dill. Set a heavy weight on top of the fish. Cover and refrigerate for two days turning the salmon every 12 hours.

3 For the mustard sauce, place the egg yolks, seasoning, sugar and half the vinegar and mustard into a food processor fitted with a metal blade and chop.

4 Gradually add the oil in a steady stream onto the running blade of the food processor until the sauce thickens. Stir in the remaining vinegar, mustard and dill.

5 Drain the liquid from the salmon and pat dry. Cut into thin slices and serve with the mustard sauce.

Tapenade

This pungent sauce is one of the rare cases where fish marries well with beef. The saltiness of the anchovies has been diffused by the olives, oil and garlic.

Serves 4

INGREDIENTS
3 lb trimmed fillet of beef
large bunch of fresh rosemary
4 garlic cloves, crushed
1¼ cups olive oil
salt and freshly ground black pepper

For the tapenade
2 oz canned anchovies
¾ cup pitted black olives
2 garlic cloves
2 egg yolks
⅔ cup olive oil
2 tsp lemon juice

egg

rosemary

black olives

beef fillet

garlic

anchovies

1 In a non-metallic dish cover the beef with the rosemary, garlic cloves, oil and seasoning. Leave to marinate for at least 2 hours in the refrigerator.

2 For the tapenade, drain the anchovies and leave them to soak in a bowl of cold water for about 20 minutes.

3 In a food processor fitted with a metal blade, roughly chop the anchovies, olives and garlic cloves.

4 Add the egg yolks and gradually pour in the oil while the blades are still running.

5 Stir in the lemon juice and season to taste. Chill for 30 minutes.

6 Spread the tapenade over the beef and cook in an oven preheated to 375°F for 45 minutes. Serve sliced with a crisp green salad.

Classic Fish Pie

Instead of a potato topping the fish base could be topped with puff pastry. Simply cook at 375°F for 30–40 minutes until golden brown.

Serves 6

INGREDIENTS
1 lb mixed raw seafood fish such as cod or salmon fillets and peeled shrimp
finely grated rind of 1 lemon
1 lb potatoes
salt and freshly ground black pepper

For the sauce
3 tbsp butter
1 tbsp plain flour
⅔ cup milk
3 tbsp chopped fresh parsley
1 egg

parsley

milk

shrimp

butter

salmon fillet

cod fillet

flour

lemon

potato

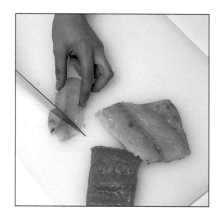

1 Preheat the oven to 425°F. Grease a 2 cups ovenproof dish. Cut the fish into bite-sized pieces.

2 Season the fish, sprinkle over the lemon and place in the base of the dish.

3 Cook the potatoes in boiling, salted water until tender.

4 Meanwhile, make the sauce. Melt 1 tbsp butter in a saucepan, add the flour and cook for a few minutes. Remove from the heat and gradually whisk in the milk. Return to the heat and bring to a boil. Simmer, whisking all the time, until the sauce has thickened. Add the parsley and season to taste. Pour over the fish.

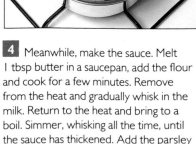

5 Drain and mash the potatoes adding the remaining butter.

6 Pipe or spoon the potatoes on top of the fish mixture. Beat the egg and brush over the potato. Bake in the preheated oven for 45 minutes until the top is golden brown.

Bouillabaise

A classic French soup containing a mixture of fish.

Serves 6

INGREDIENTS

3 lb white fish with heads such as
   monkfish, pollock, red mullet,
   whiting, bass, red snapper, perch or
   haddock
2 lb oily fish with heads such as
   mackerel, eel or striped bass
2 large crabs
8 lobster tails
¾ cup olive oil
2 medium onions, sliced
2 leeks, trimmed and sliced
2 celery stalks, sliced
1 lb tomatoes, peeled, deseeded and
   chopped
3 garlic cloves, crushed
bouquet garni
thinly peeled strip of orange rind
2 sprigs fresh fennel
5 cups fish stock
pinch of saffron strands steeped in
   2 tbsp boiling water
1 tbsp tomato paste
1 tbsp Pernod
salt and freshly ground black pepper
3 tbsp chopped fresh parsley
1 loaf French bread, thinly sliced

For the marinade
3 tbsp olive oil
2 garlic cloves, finely chopped
pinch of saffron strands steeped in
   2 tbsp boiling water
chopped fresh parsley, to garnish

1 Discard the fins, then scale, skin and clean the fish. Cut the fish into chunks. Use the fish heads and tails to make the fish stock.

2 To make the marinade, in a bowl mix together the olive oil, garlic and saffron. Pour this over the fish.

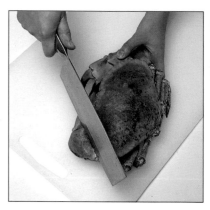

3 Leave all the shellfish in their shells. With a cleaver chop the crabs into pieces.

celery

garlic

tomato

crab

orange rind

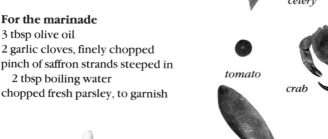

leeks

white fish

onion

oily fish

4 In a very large flameproof casserole, heat the oil and sauté the onions, leeks and celery until soft. Add the tomatoes, garlic, bouquet garni, orange rind and fennel. Stir in the fish stock, the saffron with its liquid and season to taste. Bring to a boil and cook for 30–40 minutes. 20 minutes before serving, add the oily fish and shellfish and boil hard, uncovered, for 7 minutes. Shake the pan to prevent sticking. Put the white fish on top and boil for 5 minutes longer. Discard the bouquet garni, orange rind and fennel sprigs.

5 Whisk the tomato paste and Pernod, swirl into the broth. Season well. Serve the bouillabaise in two bowls, one for the fish and one for the broth and garnish both with chopped fresh parsley. Serve with French bread.